HOPE IS EVERYTHING
By
Carolyn Terry

*Hope anchors the Soul,
Love,
Carolyn
Isa. 26:3*

BAKER BOOKS

Cover design: Carolyn Terry
ISBN: 9798841142539

Statement of Purpose

A plethora of scriptural nuggets presented in personal experience. Carolyn has overcome grief, disappointment, tragedy, loneliness, despair, confusion, and virtually every other emotional and tumultuous circumstance one must endure with the loss of a bright aspiring, Godly son. Victim of a senseless murder with neither rhyme nor reason.

As a final caregiver for a beautiful, dedicated and Spirit filled Oncology nurse, courageously battling brain cancer. Carolyn prayed day and night for her daughter to be healed as promised in the scripture. When LeAne could no longer maintain and succumbed to the final enemy Carolyn washed her face, applied a dab of make-up, praised the Lord and learned how to live while overwhelmingly missing her loved ones.

She poured all the love and vision she has accumulated over decades of following Christ into these life changing pages for anyone who has lost hope or feels the pangs of sorrow. She helps the fallen look to the hills from whence comes their help.

Chuck Baker, publisher

Introduction

May the God of hope fill you with all joy and peace in believing, so that by the power of the Holy Spirit you may abound in hope.
Romans 15:13

Be still and hope! As we look at white clouds in a blue sky or walk by a beautiful lake or ocean, our eyes are opened to His greatness and majesty. The more we understand the heart of the Father, the more our own heart will walk in hope no matter our situation or what the news media tells us. We live a short while, but we always need to remember His Kingdom is forever. We should invest in what is forever.

Since the horrible murder of my young son David, my favorite word has been Hope. My hope as a child of God is always present. As we travel through life's journey, may we stop and hope in Him. We will never waste time doing so. When our days get too busy and demanding, let us stop and rest. Just be still and rest in the shadow of His wings and be reminded of our eternal hope.

O my child,
There is a place of quiet rest
Near to the heart of God
A place where sin cannot molest
Near to the heart of God

She is clothed with strength
and dignity, she can laugh
at the days to come.
Proverbs 31:25

Carolyn Terry

To Pastor Terry Bates
OKC Faith Church
Oklahoma City, Oklahoma
Thank you for your godly wisdom, creative spirit, boundless encouragement, and unfailing friendship.
It was on your 50 days of Unleashing Hope for OKC sermons that the Holy Spirit inspired me to write this book. I am thankful.

Dedicated to Adie and Niko and to my Home School Co-op students. You are my gifts and I love making memories with you. You make my heart so happy, and I'm so blessed to call you mine. Also, to every child I have ever taught

To Dena for letting her light shine.

In honor and memory of Goldie Alley, my sister and friend, you are missed greatly. I wish you were here; however, I know you are living the eternal hope of Heaven, we always prayed for and shared. Thank you for your constant trust and faith in our Saviour. I will always be Hope and you are Faith, our nicknames for each other.

A thank you to Cecil Wilber for coming through for me again. I appreciate and love you.

Psalm 31:2

Be strong and take heart, all you who hope in the Lord.

Hope – my favorite word.

Are you looking for hope? I have promises to help you. Read on! Promises truly are the hope of the heart, and God always keeps His promises.

Standing on the promises that cannot fail, when the howling storms of doubt and fear assail, by the Word of God, I shall prevail. Standing on the promises of God. - Carter

If anyone had reason to wonder if God could or would keep His promises, it was Abraham. In Romans 4:18, we read "who against hope believed in hope, that he might become the Father of many nations, according to that

which was spoken, so shall thy seed be."
Verse 20 – He staggered not at the promise
of God through unbelief; but was strong in
faith, giving glory to God.

God alone can fill our lives with hope
and meaning. When there seems to be no
hope, He gives hope. In Psalm 119:81, we
read, "My soul faints for your salvation, but I
hope in your Word." The definition of hope
in Noah Webster's 1828 American Dictionary
of the English Language is "Full of
expectation. To desire with expectation of
good, or a belief that it may be obtained.
Confidence in a future event as a hope
founded on God's gracious promises. The
Lord will be the hope of His people. Joel
3:16." Wow! Mr. Noah Webster in 1828
dared to bring God into this definition of
hope. Today if you google this word, what
will you read?
If you are not hopeful, you are
hopeless. That is a very sad place to be. The
definition of hopeless is destitute, having no

expectation of anything good. No ground of hope or expectations. I shall be using Hebrews 11:1 many times in this book. It says, "Faith is the substance of things hoped for, the evidence of things not seen."

Please read this scripture over and over. Meditate on it – tear it apart. Faith is – the substance of things hoped for. What is faith? The substance of things hoped for and if you read down to verse 6, we read "But without faith it is impossible to please him: for he that comes to God must believe that he is and that he is a rewarder of them that diligently seek him."

Faith moves God, but you can't see it, it's the evidence of things not seen. I would always ask myself if I could see faith why would it be faith? It is the substance of things hoped for. My friends, you must never lose your hope. In times of trouble, bad reports, you must maintain your hope.

I Corinthians 13:7

Love bears all things, believes all things, hopes all things, endures all things.

We hope all things! When Paul wrote letters to the churches, he never failed to bring in the word hope. It's right in there beside love and faith. So, it must be a needful thing to get us through our journey here on earth. "Therefore, I live for today, certain of finding at sunrise, guidance and strength for the way. Power for each moment of weakness, **hope** for each moment of pain, comfort for every sorrow, sunshine and joy after rain" -Anonymous

When I think about God's love, I tend to think about all the good things He has done for me. Then I stop and know that even when life became very unfair and circumstances have been very hard, or my way was unclear, God was surrounding me with His love. God's love is just as real and just as powerful in the darkness as it is in the light. And that is why we can have hope. The day after my son, David, was murdered at a car wash in Oklahoma City, my daughter, LeAne, asked a pastor where was God when David was shot. The answer was clear, God was right there with David, because He loved David. And you know, dearest family and friends, this pastor was correct. God was right there with my son. Every day, I turn to the scriptures to give me strength and wisdom for the day and hope for the future. Its' words have seen me through good times and bad, through times of happiness and deep grief, health and sickness, victory and disappointment. God's Word, in His great love, can do the same for you.

My prayer, as I write this book, is that God will use these scriptures to encourage you and give you hope. May they cause you to trust Jesus each day and to trust His great love – no matter what comes your way. I realize there are countless books written on Hope. However, I feel the Holy Spirit leading me to write. Some of you reading this book will know me and the trials and storms I have weathered and some of you do not know me. Thank you for reading my life of this word called Hope. "Looking for that blessed hope, and the glorious appearing of the great God and our Saviour Jesus Christ. Titus 2:13.

A friend is the hope of the heart.

Ralph Waldo Emerson

Psalm 39:7

And now, Lord, what do I wait for; My hope is in you.

When the going gets tough, we must resist the temptation to give up on life, or to find ourselves complaining. Sadness and sorrow will meet us during our journey here on earth. Yes, sorrow will visit us all in some form. Read the above scripture again. No matter how tragic our lives may be, no matter if you are given to depression and despair rather than happiness and joy, we are NEVER left hopeless.

First, you must know Jesus Christ as your personal Saviour, you then can know and keep in memory that God, our loving Father will keep you by His love, mercy and grace. There are people today that can't seem to smile. I can see hopelessness and hardness on their faces. They are without hope. No wonder it's hard for them to smile.

On the other side, I see people who have overcome their trials and sorrows with a smile on their faces. They are joyful in hope. Their faces reflect the joy that is in their hearts because they have trusted in Jesus Christ. Knowing that they will dwell forever with the Lord in the place He has prepared, they continue in being joyful in hope, patient in affliction and faithful in prayer. This is hard depending upon what you are suffering, but you can do it. He did it, others down thru the ages have done it and you can do it today! Paul wrote to the Philippians and said "I can do all things through Christ who strengthens me." Did he say some things? He said, all things.

I have found that hope in the heart puts a smile on the face. Because of our faith in Christ, we can be filled with joy and hope.

I must mention here that you must not put your hope in the world. It is not to be found in human efforts, the government, the president, or any social peace messages. Only God has complete control. Quit watching the news and believing it. God knows all things. He created all things.

The prophet Isaiah said that someday "nation shall not lift up sword against nation, neither shall they learn war any more." Isaiah 2:4. The Lord Jesus Himself returns as "King of Kings and Lord of Lords" I Timothy 6:15 to set up His kingdom of peace and righteousness. I quote Titus 2:13 again. "Looking for the blessed hope and glorious appearing of our great God and our Saviour Jesus Christ."

Pastor Bates at OKC Faith Church preached "50 days of Unleashing Hope". He gave us wrist bands that reads Hold on, Pain ends. HOPE. Because we have this hope, we can trust and carry on. With hope, faith, and love we carry on. At funerals, the grieving are looking for comfort. Their loved one have died and they need comfort. What comfort do you have to offer the grieving family? Sooner or later someone dear to us will die, and we'll want to be comforted. We are hurting. I hurt so bad when my son David, 26 years old was shot to death and I spent the next 2 years in a courtroom and my young beautiful daughter died of melanoma after having 4 brain surgeries, my own precious mother died in my arms. It hurts! A hug, a kind deed, shared tears, and the presence of a friend may ease sorrow's pain just a bit. But there is always more we need when no one is around. What's beyond the grave? Will we be reunited in Heaven?

For the answers, we look to our Saviour Jesus Christ. He is the one who defeated sin and death by dying on the cross for us and rising from the grave. I Corinthians 15:1-28, 57. Because He lives, all who put their faith in Him will live forever with Him. John 11:25. In life and death, our only hope is Jesus. Paul wrote to the Thessalonians, "I do not want you to be ignorant, brethren concerning those who have fallen asleep, lest you sorrow as others who have no hope.

I Thess. 4:13. God gives us this bright ray of hope even in death.

Your words of hope to the hopeless can go a long way. My friend Geletta was shopping in a store one day and the Holy Spirit spoke to her to talk with a homeless man. He told her of his hopeless life and he is now living on the street. Geletta told him her story. Her daughter was killed in a car crash a few months before and her beloved husband has been delivered bad news from their doctor. As she related this story, she mentioned she had never started up a conversation with a homeless person ever before. She obeyed the Holy Spirit directing her to do so. What did she give this man? The word is hope. She gave him hope even when her heart was hurting. That is hope!

Romans 8:24-25

For we are saved by hope: but hope that is seen is not hope: for what a man sees, why does he yet hope for? But if we hope for that we see not, then do we with patience wait for it.

This my friends, I call a future form of faith. There was never a night or a problem that could defeat sunrise or hope. We read in Proverbs 13, hope deferred makes the heart sick, but a desire fulfilled is a tree of life. Hope is the poor man's bread.

Most people have heard of "The Adventures of "Tom Sawyer" and "Huckleberry Finn". These books were written by Mark Twain. But do you know the history of his life. I read where he had his share of tragedy. He blamed himself for his younger brother's death in a steamboat accident at age 20, and for the death of his only son, who died from diphtheria at 19 mos. He grieved bitterly over the deaths of two of his daughters. But instead of turning to God, Mr. Twain became bitter. When he died at 74, he was desperately lonely, unhappy, and hopeless. Mark Twain had an emptiness that could not be satisfied with money and fame. Hope is there, but he turned from it, weighing in only on his losses.

On the flip side, there was a man named Horatio G. Spafford, an attorney, heavily invested in real estate. When Chicago was destroyed by fire in 1871, Mr. Spafford lost a fortune. About that time, his only son, age 4 died to scarlet fever. He busied his self in rebuilding the city and assisting the 100,000 people who had been left homeless. In November, 1873, he decided to take his wife and four daughters to Europe to visit the evangelist D.L. Moody and take a vacation. His wife and four daughters went ahead of him on a luxurious French Liner. He would join them later.

On November 22, 1873 the ship collided with an iron sailing vessel. Within two hours, the luxurious French Liner vanished beneath the waters. The 226 fatalities included all of his four daughters. His wife was found clinging to a piece of the wreckage. When the 47 survivors landed in Wales, she cabled her husband which read "Saved alone".

The story goes, Horatio immediately booked passage to join his wife. Enroute, on a cold December night, the captain called him aside and said, "I believe we are passing over the place where the Liner went down". Spafford went to his cabin and wrote these words, "It is well". He later wrote his famous hymn based on these words. The first verse is:

When peace like a river attendeth my way, when sorrow like sea billows roll; whatever my lot, you have taught me to say, "It is well, it is well with my soul"

This is my favorite hymn. I love to sing this song. Now I ask you what is the difference in these two men I just told you about. Yes, Mr. Twain was hopeless and Mr. Spafford had hope. Mr. Spafford trusted Christ for salvation and looked to Him for comfort and fulfillment. It's called hope.

Have life's hardships left you feeling empty and bitter, or have they strengthened your relationship with God and made you better. Turn in faith to Jesus Christ and the God of hope will fill you with all joy and peace. Romans 15:13. Life trials should make us better, not bitter. The sun that hardens clay to brick can soften wax to shape and mold; So too, life's trials will harden some, while others purify as gold.

What oxygen is to the lungs, such is hope to the meaning of life

Emil Brunner

Romans 15:4

For whatsoever things were written before were written for our learning, that we through patience and comfort of the scripture might have hope.

I read of an old legend of an angel who was sent by God to inform Satan that all his methods to defeat Christians would be taken from him. The devil pleaded to keep just one. "Let me keep depression", he begged. The angel, thinking this a small request, agreed. "Good!" Satan exclaimed. He laughed and said, "In that one gift, I have secured all".

Depression can lead you in deep hopeless despair, you feel trapped. The prophet, Elijah cried out in I Kings 19:4. He said, "It is enough! Now Lord take my life." Job and David knew the agony of their souls, but they decided to trust God and came out with stronger faith. So encouraging to me.

Depression can come from different sources. Spiritual, mental, or physical and you should seek help. Satan would love to defeat us by keeping us in our hope-starved condition. Our biggest help is in God. He loves us and wants to shine His light through those dark clouds that surrounds us. He is the God of hope. No one is hopeless who knows the God of hope. There is hope!!

Hope is faith's companion, the encouragement on the journey. Faith sees new possibilities and hope takes us to them. Hope can stir you up to overcome fear. Hope says keep going. With faith and hope, we can move mountains. We can say no to ongoing discouragements, because we can take on hope. Find a friend whose hand you can hold on. Jesus has a big hand you can hold on to.

It doesn't matter that you don't always know where you are going. By faith, you just hold on to the master's hand, because He knows the way. He is the way, the truth, and the life.

I know today that I can have the confidence and comfort of a little girl holding on to her mother's hand leading her to safety, by me holding on to the mighty hand of the Creator, my Maker and Saviour. If I trust Him to keep me, I will get to that place, provided I never let go of the hand. My friend Brenda Cover expresses it this way. After she signs her name, she always writes "In His Hands". She knows as long as she stays in His hands, she can cast all her cares to Jesus, because He cares for her. I Peter 5:7.

His Hands healed the sick so that we could know the compassion...

His Hands held a child so that we could know His kindness...

His Hands touched the oppressed so that we could know His concern.

His Hands bore two nails so that we could know His love.

Charles Spurgeon wrote, "faith goes up the stairs that love has made and looks out of the windows which hope has opened.

The director of a medical clinic told of a terminally ill young man who came in for his usual treatment. A new doctor who was on duty said to him casually and cruelly, "You know, don't you, that you won't live out the year?" As the young man left, he stopped by the director's desk and wept. "That man took away my hope", he blurted out. "I guess he did", replied the director, "Maybe it's time to find a new one."

My comment on this incident "Is there a hope when hope is taken away? Is there hope when the situation is hopeless? That question leads us to Christian hope, for in the Bible, hope is no longer a passion for the possible. It becomes a passion for the promise. Jeremiah wrote in Chapter 17, verse 7, blessed is the man who trusts in the Lord, and whose hope is the Lord. Because God is the God of hope, He alone keeps hope flowing. The secret of coping is hoping in God. Remember the old hymn, "My hope is built on nothing less than Jesus' blood and righteousness, I dare not trust the sweetest frame, but wholly lean on Jesus' name". - Mote

Anticipating what God has in store for us can put a smile in our heart. Hope gives us inner strength, because we know that one day we will be different than we are now. Live today with the courage God gives you. Make what you can of your afflictions. If you have a living hope in Christ, you can deal with your past, because of your future. I saw my beautiful young daughter Le Ane do this as she lay dying. She had such glorious trust and faith and hope in her Saviour. We have a living hope. Blessed be God who according to His abundant mercy has begotten us again to a living hope. I Peter 1:3.

I Peter 3:15

But sanctify the Lord God in your hearts: and be ready always to give an answer to every man that asks you a reason of the hope that is in you with strength and fear

I want to do this! I choose to answer everyone the reason my heart is full of hope with strength and fear. I was in my twenties. It was a Thursday night in November, I had just put my young son, Mike, and young daughter, Le Ane, to bed. I heard the words, "You there, if you died tonight, where would you go?" It startled me, but I knew I had to answer. I was a nice person, but I knew God was dealing with me. In one shattering moment I saw my own sin. I was crushed, broken, terrified until I also saw the great love of God, and His power to forgive and purify me. I John 1:9. I fell to my knees and His presence was so real right there in my home, and I gave myself to Him. I have never

39

turned back. My hope has always been in Jesus, through all the trouble and heartache I have encountered. God reveals His holiness not to destroy us, but to expose and remove our sin. God has both an all-seeing eye and an all-forgiving heart. If you are reading this small book today and you do not know this great truth, ask Him to cleanse you today. Dear Lord, reveal to me my sin, show me the filth that dwells within; cleanse me and take my guilt away, that I may do your work this day.

Some people lose hope easy, because their eyes and mind are on the wrong things. William Wordsworth wrote, "The world is too much with us." He meant that too often we get caught up in the world's mad rush and fail to appreciate God's creation. But it's also easy to feel that the world is too much with us when we see people suffer for their faith in God. I read the tragic story of a missionary family in India devastated by the murder of the father and two sons at the hands of people who hate

Christians. Stories like this happens... It can overwhelm us when we hear all the bad news. Added to these stories could be your own account of unjust treatment of our faith.

I am no exception. I know what it's like to have a young Christian son, David, murdered at age twenty-six. I led my son to the Lord Jesus when he was only four years old. He grew up serving God. It's what he knew. He went to nursing homes, Children's Hospital, the inner city with our family to serve the Lord. He graduated from Bible College with a Bible degree. He had his master's degree. He had prepared his life to totally serve people. Then one Wednesday night after sitting in church with us, he was shot down at a car wash only 3 miles from our home. The young man who murdered my son was full of hate. Yes, it was a hate crime. No amount of words could console me. I spent the next two years in a courtroom. I know the hurt, the heartache, and the despair. And I can say thank God, I kept my hope. I believe you can lose faith and trust for a season, but you can never lose hope. This is the reason that hope is my favorite word and I'm writing this book.

We have the hope that comes from being God's children. Romans 8:16-17. We can call our Creator, "Abba Father" (v 15). We have His promise of future glory – a glory that far over-shadows "the suffering of this present time" (v 18).

Are the burdens of this world too much with you? Look to your Heavenly Father. He loves you. How do I know? He showed His love and sent us His only son to die for us. He lovingly offers help and hope to His struggling children if we let Him. No one is hopeless who knows the God of hope. There is coming a day when no heartaches shall come, no more clouds in the sky, no more tears to dim the eye; all is peace forevermore on that happy golden shore – "What a day, glorious day that will be!" - Hill

The more we think of our loving God, His word, and His promises, the less we will fret over the troubles of this world. Yes, it's a tough world, but with God we can be victorious. And everyone that has this hope in him purifieth himself, even as he is pure. I John 3:3.

God is more interested in your future and
your relationship than you are.

Billy Graham

Romans 15:13

May the God of hope fill you with all joy and peace in believing, that you may abound in hope.

It is well-known that our emotions can have an effect on our bodies. And the condition of our bodies can affect our emotions. For example, an article in the American Heart Association points to the negative physical consequences of hopelessness. It said that those who had experienced extreme feelings of despair had a 20-percent greater increase in arteriosclerosis (hardening of the arteries) over a four-year period.

This finding is not new. In the Old Testament book of Proverbs, we read that "a merry heart does good, like medicine" (17:22) and that the wisdom found in God's words "are life to those who find them, and health to all their flesh" (4:22). Health-giving hope, I call it. Hope in the heart puts a smile on the face.

The prophet Jeremiah words this in a letter to the Jewish exiles in Babylon. "For I know the plans I have for you, declares the Lord, plans for welfare and not for evil, to give you a future and a hope. Jeremiah 29:11. God had not forgotten them. He also has not forgotten you if you are reading this small book. Maybe today you find yourself in some type of misery, feeling defeated and desperate. Don't give up. You have hope in God.

Your Lord has not forgotten you. You can be sure of that. Your Heavenly Father wants only the best for you. You say, Carolyn, how can you be so sure of that. I am very sure, because God gave up His only son who died for you. That's how I know. You are worth the blood of Jesus. He is at work, even now, on your behalf. Our Lord is always faithful, even when we are not. Paul wrote in Philippians 4:6 that we are not to be anxious about anything, but in everything by prayer and supplication with thanksgiving let your requests be made known to God.

How would you define worry? One way I think about it is when we worry, we are thinking on the devil's lies. We think about all the things that could go wrong. I think it was Mark Twain that said, "I've had a lot of worries in my life, most of which never happened." I believe that worry is a sin. Pray and give it to God! You can be concerned about situations, but don't make yourself sick by worry. I have seen some people who would rather worry and complain than pray and believe God for the best. Philippians 4:7 tells us, "And the peace of God, which passes all understanding shall keep your hearts and mind in Christ Jesus. Be positive and not negative all the time. I think the real question we should ask ourselves is do I believe God or do I not believe God. Are we believers or not?

A man named Benjamin Franklin said, "Early to bed, early to rise would make a man healthy, wealthy, and wise." Still today, most people want to be healthy, some want to be wealthy, but wise? Really? Yes really!! Get wisdom, and understanding God values wisdom and understanding. "The fear of the Lord is the beginning of wisdom: and the knowledge of the Holy is understanding." Proverbs 9:10. Reverence for God, knowing Him deeply and personally – this is wisdom. This kind of respect and relationship comes only thru faith in His son, Jesus Christ. God gave! So knowing all this, can't we trust Him and not worry ourselves. I wait for the Lord, my soul waits and in His word I hope. Psalm 130:5.

At times, we feel our strength is all gone, but God promises that even at our lowest point, even when we feel there is nothing left, He is there to offer us hope. We all experience "alone" at some time in our lives. It is natural. In those times, we can discover that we are never truly alone. I have learned that people who seem to have it all, are living in despair with no hope, because they feel so alone. So many people are committing suicide. So many young people. Why? They are tricked into believing the devil's lies that they are all alone.

My son had a very close friend in high school. They played basketball together. This young friend to our family was only 20 years old, when they found his body. He had put a gun in his mouth and pulled the trigger. All of us grieved. My son grieved the death of his close friend Eric. His mother grieved. Why, we all asked ourselves. He was in our home just days before. We loved him. Why? The answer has to be he had lost all hope. And he believed lies instead of truth. Dear God, lead me by your truth and teach me for you are the God who saves me. All day long I put my hope in you. Psalm 25:5.

Dear reader, please remember your source of hope. It's the song of a bird, snow covered mountains, the roar of the ocean, a spring flower coming out of the snow, the stars in the sky. These are all wonders that points us to God, the source of all hope.

They, to me, are reminders that no poverty, pain, sickness, disappointments, grief, even our own death can steal our hope when it is firmly rooted in God. I choose to believe His promises. I have walked thru the dark, confusing, lonely, and painful places. I have buried my precious son and daughter. I have been very sick and I know what it's like to have no money. I also know the perfect peace I have had. His promises replaced my clouds of despair with a light of God's love. Thank you for a voice to sing your praises with my whole heart. Thank you Jesus for hope.

Job 17:15

And where is now my hope? As for my hope who shall see it?

"Pictures of Hope"

While visiting relatives in a rural area, a father decided to take a night walk with the young daughter. The father could hardly wait to show his daughter a star filled sky. As dusk turned into dark, she looked toward the sky and exclaimed, "Daddy, somebody drew dots all over the sky." Her father smiled. His daughter had never seen a night sky away from the city lights. "Daddy", she continued in her enthusiasm, "if we connect them all, will they make a picture?" The night sky had taken on the quality of a dot-to-dot puzzle for his child! What an interesting notion, the father thought. "No", he replied to his daughter, "the dots are there for another purpose. Each one is a hope God has for your life. God loves you so much, He has lots of hopes that your life will be filled with good things. In fact, there are more hopes than you or I can even count!"

"I knew it!" the little girl gasped. "The dots do make a picture." And then she added more thoughtfully, "I always wondered what hope looked like."

When God showed Abraham the stars and asked him to count them, He was giving him hope that the promise He had made to him – that he would have a son – was coming. Genesis 15:5. Whenever the sky is clear at night, do what I do, go outside and stand in your driveway and lift your hands to God in Heaven. Praise Him with your voice and your heart. I have done this for years. The powerful Creator who put these stars in place will hear your praises and see you. Wow, when my heart was troubled the most, I would stand in my driveway believing all was well in my soul. Nothing like it! It has a name. It's called Peace. Did it always change my situation? No, but it changed me.

The stars are a picture of God's hope – for you, for your family, for the world. Looking up is one of the best ways to get your earthly life in focus and realize that in God's infinite universe He has a specific plan for you, just as He did for Abraham. If you doubt this, remember Christ died for all, and that is you!

I live in Lakeview neighborhood in Oklahoma City. On a December 8th, I turned into the neighborhood off N.W. Expressway onto Libby and the ball-joint on my right front tire tore off. I was barely off the Expressway and in the center of Libby. When I got out to see what the sudden, loud crash was all about and noticed my tire off, a man stopped to help me. He could see the danger I was in and he stayed with me, directing traffic for 3 hours in the cold. He changed his schedule to stay until the tow truck came and took my car away.

When I thanked him and asked his name. He said Hope! I was taken back and moved to tears. What Mr. Hope didn't know about me was that my young son, David, was murdered at a car wash a few years before and "hope" became my favorite word.

I thought of all the people in the city, God sent me help named "Hope". His kindness and help and staying with me in the cold weather until my car was towed away. This is a picture of hope. Thank you my Heavenly Father. So many pictures of hope if we had an eye or ear to see and hear.

Faith goes up the stairs that love has built and looks out the window which hope has opened.

Charles H Spurgeon

Romans 12:12

Rejoicing in hope; patient in tribulation; continuing instant in prayer.

Pray with hope

When we pray, do we know for certain that God hears us. Jesus is life and He has overcome darkness. We can ask according to His will and He does hear us. We have to know in our heart Jesus is truth. His truth has broken every lie, so we can pray with confidence, knowing that He hears. His power has torn down every bondage, so we can pray with freedom. His love has conquered every fear, so we can pray with hope.

There are prayers and promises in the Bible. Paul wrote Colossians 1:3-5 "We give thanks to God and Father of our Lord Jesus Christ, praying always for you, since we heard of your faith in Christ Jesus and of your love for all the saints; because of the hope which is laid up for you in heaven."

In Romans 15:13 – "Now may the God of hope fill you with all joy and peace in believing, that you may abound in hope by the power of the Holy Spirit."

I have found this to be true in my life. There are times when I know not what to pray for. I pray for wisdom, and He helps me. I can pray according to scripture when I don't even see how it is going to be fulfilled. Above all, I don't stop praying. Jesus makes intercession for us. Pray with the simplicity of a little child and know He hears us. We are filled with hope when we pray with our whole heart.

I want to share the following writing of my young teenage friend I met at City Rescue Mission. His name is Jeremy. I know his family. They are close to me to this very day.

How Others Prayed

Somewhere, someone is crying out
Depression causing them to shout,
For a better day.
Ending it all now is in their mind
This whole world is so unkind
So, they choose another way.

Stop, and let me tell you a story from time ago.
A lonely boy was tired of life, he said, he had no hope.
So he did careless things to end it all
He didn't care, he's tired of life, there just isn't any hope.

Then Jesus, thru the prayer of loved ones that cared all the more.
Told the boy that all of his sins Jesus already bore.
So, through it all, no matter how it seems, God is there for you.

61

You can overcome pain and strife and depression too
If only you believe you, Jesus will never leave.

Now, a blood-bought Christian boy is back, telling others of his past.
So, they can choose another way spreading the Word of our Saviour
And Lord, armed only with a two-edged sword.

AS HE REMEMBERS HOW OTHERS PRAYED

Thank you for your prayers. I love you
Jeremy

I received this letter from Jeremy. I thank God that hope lightened his load. Prayer is utmost important. Jesus himself, often withdrew to lonely places and prayed. Luke 5:15-16. Beauty lies in quiet things and they are everywhere, but we may fail to find them unless we pause for prayer. -June Masters Bacher

62

Ephesians 4:32

And be kind one to another, tenderhearted, forgiving one another, even as God for Christ's sake has forgiven you.

Forgiveness is vital if you live a full life of hope, faith, and love. I'm going to share a few words why. The word of God has made us free. We are not in bondage to anything or anyone.

We cannot be forgiven if we refuse to forgive. Jesus said, "But if you forgive not men their trespasses, neither will your Father forgive your trespasses." Matthew 6:15.

When we learn to forgive the past, we sow the seeds for a glorious future and hope. Many times hope is found in forgiveness. Paul wrote in Colossians 3:13, "Bear with each other and forgive one another if any of you has a grievance against someone. Forgive as the Lord forgave you."

I think back on a time when someone I loved broke my heart, rejected me, betrayed me, and told lies about me to protect himself. I also think back to a time when a heart full of hate shot my young son to death. A complete stranger walked up to David, called my son a bad name and just shot him for no reason. Our mind fights for retaliation. We want to make sense of it.

In time I remembered how much God forgives me. I am so thankful Jesus took my punishment and made me free. I chose forgiveness because it sets me free of any bitterness. Nothing over powers it. Forgiveness saves me from yesterday and makes one strong in the present. It shows me how much God loved me and gave His only son, Jesus.

These people did not deserve or even requested my forgiveness, but by making my decision of forgiveness I now had love, peace, and hope I had never known. In other words, it actually helps us the most when we forgive. For me, it shows the real love of my master for me and helps those watching on the sidelines. In fact, I had a Fox 25 news reporter who asked me if I had forgiven my son's killer, because she knew I was a Christian. I answered yes, it was never about unforgiveness, it's about justice.

Wrapping ourselves in bitterness is like using a blanket of poison ivy; it's warm at first but painful in the end. Ephesians 4:31 says "Let all bitterness be put away from you." I've heard it said, "If we nurture bitterness, it will destroy love; if we nurture love, it will destroy bitterness."

We will never find a scripture that says, "Jesus washed all the disciples' feet except the feet of Judas and Peter." You can be sure Jesus knew the future of the feet He was washing. These twenty-four feet will not spend the next day following their master, defending his cause. These feet will dash for cover at the flash of the Roman sword. Think about it, what a moment when Jesus lifts the feet of His betrayer, Judas, and washes them. Within hours, Judas will stand in

Caiaphas' court betraying Jesus. He knows what the others will do. He knows they will bury their heads in shame and look down at their feet. Wow, Jesus offered mercy before they even sought it. Please note here, Judas went out and hung himself with no hope, but Peter asks for forgiveness. And it was Peter who God used to bring three thousand to the Body of Christ in one day. Read it in the Book of Acts.

My point, Jesus gives us forgiveness and He gives us hope.

Hope is being able to see that there is light
despite all darkness!

Desmond Tutu

Jeremiah 17:7

Blessed is the man that trusts in the Lord, and whose hope is the Lord.

Israel's hope was always in the Lord God. God is the giver of hope. Our hope in Jesus is timeless. Why? Because He is our eternal hope. I know the hope I have found and it's in Him, the giver of hope. Think about this, if we want to share the hope we have found, we must "know" the hope we have found. I memorized Philippians 3:10 years ago. "That I might know Him and the power of His resurrection and the fellowship of His sufferings being made conformable to His death.

Are we hopeful because we know personally the giver of hope and truly believe that He has our best interests at heart? I'm not talking about the world's hope. Isaiah 40:31 says, "Those that wait upon the Lord shall renew their strength", here, I'm going to insert the word hope –

Those who hope in the Lord shall renew their strength, they will mount up on wings like eagles, they shall run and not be weary, they shall walk and not faint, teach me Lord, teach me Lord to wait or hope.

Have you ever heard someone say, "I really hope it works out!" or maybe, "I hope everything ends up okay"? This is not negative, however this kind of hope can be fickle. Here the word "hope" is used as a positive expression – a kind of like wishing that may or may not come true.

I want us to think more about biblical hope. This kind, I believe, comes from a hopeful heart. When we hope in God, we are believing it. When we hope in God, we are choosing faith. Thank you Jesus, that your hope is not one that discourages us. Your hope is always present because you are always present and you are our hope. Show us how to cling to your hope. Let us look different than the world.

Hope that can be destroyed or taken away is no hope at all, but eternal hope? It can be tested, but not destroyed. It can be questioned, but not taken away. It rests in the promises of God.

Paul wrote these words in Hebrews 6:11-12 "And we desire that everyone of you do show the same diligence to the full assurance of hope to the end: that you be not slothful, but followers of them who through faith and patience inherit the promises." What is the difference between faith and hope? Faith is the substance of things hoped for, the evidence of things not seen! Hebrews 11:1 Hope is defined as that same assuredness, but in the future.

I think we often use the word hope with a more wishy-washy meaning than faith. Hope was never meant to be used this way according to the word of God. I like this saying I heard one time (Hope is ironed-out faith) and it is certain about a situation, relationship, or happening in the future. It operates with full trust that God will show up. The reason why our hope is fickle is because we often place it in the wrong things or the wrong people. When we put hope in anything but our creator, it can easily be taken away. Disappointment can break it, insecurity can crush it, and fear can convince us to be silent.

But the hope we have? It is our faith in action. Hope and faith are intertwined, requiring one for the other. Wow, when I saw this for the first time, it was like I saw a brand new light. Because we have faith in the one who holds our today, we have hope for our future. Listen to this – It is our hope that often gives us the strength we need to continue to operate in our faith today. Hope was never meant to be a wish fountain. It is confidence that God will be God. Faith is confidence that the darkness will pass and hope continues to dream because it believes that statement of faith to be true. Hope allows us to overcome our heartaches. Hope in God can help us put aside every worry, because we trust the Lord who will never leave us. Hope in God is everything.

Dear Jesus, thank you for showing this to us. Thank you for being the author of our faith and the giver of our hope. Our hope is secure in you. Help us to get rid of our doubts, so we might become a light of hope to a lost world. Amen.

Hope is the last thing ever lost.

Italian proverb

I Thessalonians 2:19-20

For what is our hope, or joy, or crown of rejoicing? Are not even you in the presence of our Lord Jesus Christ at his coming? For you are our glory and joy.

I chose the above scripture because of the word joy. I love how the words hope and joy just seem to fit together. If you have hope in the unseen tomorrow, then joy rises up in your soul to give you strength for the journey. I have seen Christians with no joy. Sometimes the cares of this life can make us so anxious that we just see the ground. Lift your eyes. You need to remember your faith and hope. You could decide to go out of your way to cheer someone up. I have found this will lift your spirit and the joy of your salvation will rise up.

Have you ever noticed that we're naturally drawn to people who are fun to be around...people who radiate joy? They draw people naturally. If you want to win people to the Lord, kindness, and joy and hope will do it. There's something about choosing joy that fills our hearts with hope for better days ahead. The Bible teaches us that the joy of the Lord is our strength.

In Psalm 42:2-5, we read the Psalmist cry out, "Why are you downcast, O my soul? Why so disturbed within me? Put your hope in God." In the book of Acts, Paul was onboard a ship going to Rome, a storm threatened to take the ship and all onboard to the bottom of the sea. An angel of the Lord appeared and assured Paul that no one would perish. Paul's hope was in the Lord.

Remember the psalmist's words "Put your hope in God" and Paul's "I believe God". If that's not enough, mediate on Philippians 4:19 – "But my God shall supply all your need according to His riches in glory by Christ Jesus". "Keep looking unto Jesus, the author and finisher of our faith" Hebrews 12:2.

Titus 2:13-14

Looking for that blessed hope, and the glorious appearing of the great God and our Saviour Jesus Christ; who gave himself for us that He might redeem us from all sin and purify unto himself a peculiar people, zealous of good works.

There are times in my life that I have to encourage myself. I am happy to be reminded that in I Samuel 30:6, you can read these words, "And David was greatly distressed; for the people spoke of stoning him, because the soul of all people was grieved, every man for his sons and for his daughters; but David encouraged himself in the Lord". Wow! If David could, I can. And you can! There are times when no one is around and you can think of better days and hope can arise and you have encouraged yourself!

When I received Jesus as my Saviour at age 26 years old, I prayed to God to send me someone to teach me. I knew people my own age didn't have the wisdom and understanding to help me grow spiritually. I met a beautiful 80 year old lady at the Church Christian Center on North May Ave. She became my Mamma Boggs. We often think of the springtime of youth as the most beautiful time of life. The body is strong, the mind is sharp. Yet the sixties, seventies, and eighties are even more beautiful – for those who are "found in the way of righteousness" Proverbs 16:31.

In his book, The Best is Yet to Be, Henry Durbanville tells about a woman who had charm and grace that others couldn't help but notice. One day a younger woman said to her, "I think you are perfectly beautiful!" The woman quietly said, "I should be, my dear. After all, I'm 81 years old."

There is nothing like the beauty of a loving heart shining through a seasoned face. When we walk with God, the years have a way of refining us. The sufferings I have endured during my lifetime has mellowed me and reveals who I really am in Christ.

That's what I saw with my 26 year old eyes when I met my Momma Boggs. I saw beauty. She taught me for 15 years and I was privileged to be with her when she quietly entered Heaven at 95 years old. She taught me the word day by day and she lived it. I was her Carolyn. Paul wrote in 2 Corinthians 4:16, "Even though our outward man is perishing, yet the inward man is being renewed day by day".

Looking back, I never thought of Mrs. Boggs as being old. She was always happy and hopeful. I believe she determined that her older years would be gracious and pleasant and always hopeful. Some old people hang on to life's hurts with bitterness.

I found this poem – How old are you? Age is a quality of mind; If you have left your dream behind, If hope is cold, If you no longer look ahead, If your ambition fires are dead – then you are old. But if from life you take the best, And if in life you keep the jest, If love and hope you hold; No matter how the years go by, No matter how the birthdays fly, You are not old.

God called me to children after I received my Saviour Jesus. It is a high calling. I still teach children. I have my own Home School Co-op. Such a blessed privilege! My hope is in a child. I have taught thousands all over the city: churches, private schools, inner city, and hospitals. Whatever you write on the heart of a child is never lost. Time will never change it. Children know if you are real or not. I knew that what I was, was more important than what I taught. I loved, laughed, and learned right along with them. They are the hope of my life. I love them – they keep me going and fills me with hope. I teach them and they teach me with their love and hopeful hearts. They are so thankful!

I had the privilege of teaching and loving thousands of children and teens in the inner city of Oklahoma City. I was down there for 26 years teaching that Jesus is their answer from the hood, gangs, and drugs. I had a little boy that came, he grew up and today serves as the OU football chaplain. Thank you, Jesus for all these you have given me.

Isaiah 26:3

Thou will keep him in perfect peace whose mind is stayed upon thee because he trusts in thee.

I end this small book using my favorite scripture. My first book bore this scripture on the cover. Isaiah 26:3 Perfect Peace in His Presence. It is a daily devotional.

Hope is my favorite word. The Lord let me write this small book on it. I have had sufferings and hardships in my life. Everyone does. I chose love, forgiveness, trust, joy, and hope in the Lord.

I wear many hats. I'm Mom, Nana, friend, sister, aunt, teacher, minister, and more. Imagine my surprise when I was asked to be a floor designer and decorator for a store. Wow!! I accepted and I have been at Heart and Hand for four years. I love it. I love being creative. Heart and Hand is a ministry. It is a Bible-based organization that assists families, giving them a "hand up and not a hand out". Women are given hope for a future. They are encouraged to establish a relationship with God, acknowledge Him as the one who will give them a sense of self-worth and hope.

I have the privilege of working at the Heart and Hand Thrift Center. The store meets needs for the women and children. Within those walls, you can see the Power of Hope. I loved Brenda's words; the store is a ministry in itself. I'm the decorator, but I am given a go ahead to listen and pray for our customers.

Another book could be written titled, "Miracles of Hope on North West 23rd Street". Great title, Brenda, because it's true.

I work with precious people. God brings in hearts of like-faith! We work, share, love, and laugh. Our hearts and hands offer hundreds of people hope. Our customers come in to shop for good prices, however they become close friends also. We know each other's name and we get to know each other. I have prayed for them. And I have seen miracles of healing. Customers come back in and gives us testimonies of their healing, after they were prayed for in the store.

Heart – Hand – Hope

In quietness and confidence shall be your strength -Isaiah 30:15

"Add hope every day"

Unto you......which believe, He, (hope) is precious. -I Peter 2:7

In fact, hope is best gained after defeat and failure, because then inner strength and toughness are produced.

Fritz Knapp

NOTES

NOTES

NOTES

NOTES

NOTES

Made in USA - Crawfordsville, IN
60931_9798841142539
03.01.2023 1826